Fart Dictionary

Scott A. Sorensen

Illustrations by Carl Wiens

RUNNING PRESS

PHILADELPHIA

Running Press
Hachette Book Group
1290 Avenue of the Americas, New York, NY 10104
www.runningpress.com
@Running_Press

Printed in China

First Edition: August 2011

Published by Running Press, an imprint of Perseus Books, LLC, a subsidiary of Hachette Book Group, Inc. The Running Press name and logo is a trademark of the Hachette Book Group

The Hachette Speakers Bureau provides a wide range of authors for speaking events. To find out more, go to www.hachettespeakersbureau.com or call (866) 376-6591.

The publisher is not responsible for websites (or their content) that are not owned by the publisher.

Print book cover and interior design by Joshua McDonnell.

Library of Congress Control Number: 2010938757

ISBNs: 978-0-7624-9177-3 (hardcover), 978-0-7624-9176-6 (ebook)

RRD-S

10 9 8 7 6 5 4 3 2

A BRIEF INTRO

Everybody farts, even movie stars. Did you know Johnny Depp and Jennifer Aniston both own fart machines? True story. Benjamin Franklin even wrote a book titled *Fart Proudly*. Wasn't he a forefather of our country? He took time out of his busy political career to write a fart book. Makes you think, huh? I guess that makes him a fore-fart-father of the U.S.A.

The average human farts fourteen times per day, which equates to over 105 billion farts spanning our globe daily. Chances are someone near you just sent a "gift" in your general direction. We've all experienced the same old fart jokes, antics, and social discomforts. Society has compelled us to hide our most basic instincts, but farting is a human necessity we all have in common. So, readers, the next time you fart, or bear witness to one, take note of your surroundings, purpose, or social inconvenience. Label it, as I've done in this *Fart Dictionary*. From A to Z, there's something for everyone.

abandoned fart: a fart left to be enjoyed by others; i.e. elevator exit, crowded room, or your supervisor's office.

abducted fart: a fart that's claimed by someone other than the farter.

Abraham Lincoln fart: a fart released by the orator during an important speech.

absorbed fart: a fart captured by surrounding clothing that has no chance of making it into the atmosphere, most common at Chicago Bears football games in December.

abstract fart: a fart that leaves remnants resembling a Picasso.

accurate fart: a fart aimed and delivered on target in the direction of a predetermined location or individual.

acute fart: a fart with high tone and precision, not to be confused with a "cute" fart delivered by a newborn.

air-raid fart: a fart so disgusting you need to warn others immediately.

albacore fart: a fart with the faint aroma of tuna, most commonly found in small delicatessens on the outskirts of South Florida retirement villages.

alley fart: a fart delivered at the precise moment one releases the bowling ball for a strike (not to be confused with the "alley-oops fart," which only results in a spare).

ammo fart: a fart you've saved as a defensive weapon against other farters in your immediate fart zone.

amplified fart: a fart enhanced in sound level by a micro-phone (most common at late-night bachelorette karaoke parties in metropolitan Japan).

anarchic fart: a fart purposely emitted during a presidential speech.

animal Control fart: a fart that smells like a baboon has escaped the zoo and taken refuge somewhere in your house.

animated fart: a fart enhanced by the lifting of a leg, a curtsy, or a quick, gleeful dance.

anonymous fart: a fart of unknown origin when there's no dog in the immediate vicinity.

anterior fart: a fart that rises up the front of your pants as opposed to the rear. (Note: Check the tightness of your underwear without delay.)

antihistamine fart: a fart that miraculously cures the itchy rash on your rear.

anxious fart: a fart that causes the farter an extreme level of stress at the thought of what the fart may have left in their britches.

apple fart: a fart that keeps the doctor away.

Arctic-exploration fart: a fart expelled while walking your girlfriend's bladder-shy Pekingese in subzero weather.

argument fart: a fart that replaces "getting the last word in" during a disagreement.

artisan fart: any fart discharged by one who is recognized by his or her friends as a "master farter."

ask-me fart: a fart delivered in response to a stupid question.

assault fart: a fart used as an offensive weapon during a fart attack. Or, the first fart with intention to start a fart war.

at-bat fart: a fart purposely left at home plate for a near-sighted umpire.

auto-graft fart: a fart so physically disruptive, it feels like your sphincter has been displaced.

baby's-breath fart: a fart soft and shy in tone, and lacking any aroma whatsoever.

bad-blood fart: a fart most common at family reunions where the farter has no concern for another family member's immediate airspace.

bait-and-switch fart: a fart often used by furniture salesmen to get the customer to move on to a more expensive item.

bandwagon fart: a fart with such instant popularity that everyone joins in, and it soon turns into a fart festival.

banister fart: a fart delivered at the bottom of a flight of stairs, but which eventually ends up in your sister's upstairs bedroom.

baptism-of-fire fart: a deplorable fart launched at the newest member of your weekly poker game.

basic-decision fart: a fart in which you have ample time to decide on a release location.

Batman fart: the most stellar of all farts used in fart combat, recognizable by its sleek delivery and aromatic stealth. (Note: Its use for any reason other than combat may result in fart pandemonium, which could cause yet another small hole in our ozone.)

bean-pole fart: this fart occurs only when you have your shirt tightly tucked in, and the fart bubble travels upward and exits at your neckline (Note: This is sometimes mistaken for extremely bad breath.)

bench-warrant fart: a fart that you committed but have publicly denied, even though all in attendance (the fart jury) have found you unanimously guilty.

Benji fart: a fart that sounds cute, but smells bad.

Bermuda-bag fart: a fart expelled by a large female tourist while exiting down the gangplank of a Caribbean cruise ship.

bewitched fart: a fart that causes your nose to twitch.

Big Bird fart: a fart from the tallest blonde in the room.

binding fart: a fart which initiates a personal relationship due to both individuals' fart interests.

birth-control fart: a fart that will rid the area of prospective males willing to father your children.

birthstone fart: a fart you tried so hard to muster up, it feels like you're manufacturing diamonds in your digestive track.

blah-blah-blah fart: the boring person dominating the conversation has finally gone beyond your attention span, so you let loose an interruption.

boa-constrictor fart: any fart that wraps around your face and won't let go.

bob fart: a fart that arises as a single bubble without immediately popping while taking a bath.

bombastic fart: a fart that wasn't that great, but the farter won't stop bragging about it.

boomerang fart: a fart emitted with certainty of wind speed and direction, but which has somehow returned to haunt you.

Brazilian fart: a painful fart during a bikini waxing.

bread-and-butter fart: the basic fart in your fart arsenal that can be easily manufactured and relied upon for use at any time.

break-up fart: a fart used in a confined space to end a relationship.

broadside fart: a fart from another farter that hits you like a tsunami, causing you to lose your footing or grab on to a handrail for support.

broncobuster fart: a fart that makes you buck and lunge out of your chair.

bubblegum fart: a fart that feels like it never made it past your clothing and gives a feeling that there's a bubblegum bubble in your pants.

bumblebee fart: a fart that causes a sharp stinging sensation.

bungee-cord fart: a fart that comes back to you so quickly it's impossible to escape the stench evidence, and now everyone knows who let it go.

butterfingered fart: a fart you had no plans of releasing, but it just slipped right through with no warning or obvious cause.

buttermilk fart: a fart purposely left internally for an extended time, thus allowing it to cultivate with other bacteria and ultimately resulting in a heinously vile fart.

buzzard fart: a fart so smelly large birds of prey begin circling overhead.

cable-guy fart: a fart that always comes later than you expect it to.

calcium-chloride fart: you've eaten so many antacids to control your gastric tension that all your farts now smell like Rolaids.

call-box fart: a fart let go in a moving vehicle that's so stomach turning you must pull over and allow all passengers to exit and catch their breath.

Candy Crush fart: a fart you can't stop playing with long after you've farted.

Castro fart: a fart that smells like a bad cigar.

cauliflower fart: judging by the air mass you've just released, you're prepared for a real stinker, but no, it's harmless.

central-air fart: a fart purposely disposed of very near the intake of an HVAC unit.

cheapskate fart: a fart used to redirect the course of the collection plate at church as it nears you.

chicken-sausage fart: a fart saved to present to your butcher in order to prove to him, without a doubt, he sold you some really bad sausage last night.

classical fart: a symphonic fart in stereo.

closet fart: a fart by an individual who claims to have never farted in public.

contagious fart: a fart that spawns one of the same pitch and aroma from another person in the room.

coronation fart: a fart released at the precise moment a new king is crowned.

Cover Girl fart: a fart you left in the makeup aisle at WalMart.

crop-rotation fart: the second half of a particularly smelly fart you saved for the other side of the room.

cross-pollination fart: a fart created when two farts become one.

Custer fart: your last fart before being kicked out of an Indian casino.

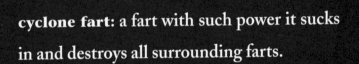

cyclone fart: a fart with such power it sucks in and destroys all surrounding farts.

danke-schoen fart: a fart used at the end of a Vegas floor show in lieu of applause.

dark-horse fart: a fart expelled by an individual you wouldn't expect to win the fart contest.

Darwinian fart: a fart which only the fittest survive.

dead-cat fart: a fart with nine discernible layers of foulness.

dead-end fart: a fart you mistakenly released at the end of a hallway or corridor, and now there's no means of escape.

"Dear Abby" fart: a fart that causes uncomfortable unrest to your entire household.

Del Monte fart: a fart let go in the canned vegetable aisle while deciding if the more expensive can of beans will result in better farts.

diagnostic fart: a fart you saved for your doctor so he can decide what exactly it is that ails you.

ding-dong fart: a fart you let go before answering the front door to save yourself the embarrassment of farting in front of company.

dispensary fart: a fart in the marijuana store which causes a line to form around the building to purchase the new strain they smell.

dinner-guest fart: you thought you left your fart in the bathroom, but no, it followed you all the way back to the dining table.

downward-facing-dog fart: a fart let go during yoga class.

drive-thru fart: a fart so loud it can be heard through the speaker at the fast food drive-up, thus resulting in total embarrassment, and the passenger in your car makes you leave immediately.

dry-heave fart: an uncontrollable fart let go while hugging the toilet after a session of all-night partying.

dust-bunny fart: a fart emitted while hiding under your sister's bed.

dynamic-duo fart: a fart from the sugar-overdosed, caped twins ringing your doorbell on Halloween.

Eagle Scout fart: a fart emitted by a farter held in high regard by his farting peers, primarily because of his reputation as a "straight and self-reliant farter."

Easter-egg fart: a particularly nasty, egg-fragranced fart, but with a hint of smoked ham as it settles.

Eastwood fart: a fart that makes your day.

easy-mark fart: a fart ejected onto an unsuspecting victim, most commonly the person next to you in bed or your dog.

economic-stimulus fart: any fart that immediately sends you out to shop for new underwear.

elevator fart: one that causes your ears to pop.

El Niño fart: an unusually warm fart that drifts across the pool.

Elmo fart: a fart that tickles your butt.

end-zone fart: a celebratory fart released by a tight end after making a touchdown.

entitled fart: a fart that confuses millennials.

exit-backwards fart: a fart which leads you to leave the room without turning around for fear of what others may see on the backside of your pants.

face-mask fart: a fart delivered "for your eyes only" by the person in front of you at a crowded, indoor, assigned-seating event.

Facebook fart: a fart of such popularity it's shared and liked by billions of people you've never met.

failure-to-communicate fart: a fart from a six-year-old signaling he's not paying attention to your lecture on why he can't pee in the grocery-store parking lot.

failure-to-launch fart: a fart a forty-year-old living in his parents' basement lets loose, in an attempt to get himself some privacy.

fireside fart: you're having a rendezvous in front of the fireplace and one of you lets go a gas cloud, which causes a fireball to jump out of the embers and almost sets the ceiling ablaze.

first-date fart: it's too soon in the relationship to kiss her goodnight, so you settle for a firm hug and oops, she farts.

fly-swatter fart: a fart in public that earns you a slap on the butt from mom.

food-fight fart: a fart that causes the person you're eating lunch with to throw their meatball sandwich at you.

frisbee fart: a fart that quietly glides across the room, going unnoticed by everyone but the dog.

frog-leg fart: a fart that smells just like chicken.

Fruit of the Loon fart: any fart emitted while in a canoe that's thunderous enough to get a response from nearby waterfowl.

fruitcake fart: a fart that no one likes.

gadget fart: a fart with a mechanical sound. (You can pretend it came from your preschooler's toy box.)

galactic fart: a painful fart that makes you see stars.

game-ball fart: an awarded fart for masterful fart exhibition, which brought victory to your fart team.

Game of Thrones fart: a fart you've been anticipating all week long to find out what it smells like.

gargoyle fart: a mythological fart said to turn the farter into stone.

gene-pool fart: a fart that reminds you of your dad.

gentile fart: a fart expelled by a Catholic at a bar mitzvah.

get-out-the-banjo fart: a fart so rhythmic in composition it could very well become the melody for a country music tune about a lonely guy and his lactose intolerant mother-in-law.

goaltending fart: a fart used to cordon off a room to discourage others from entering.

gold-digger fart: a fart used to extort money from another.

good-impression fart: a fart delivered purposely for the person in your immediate social zone with prior knowledge of their love of farts.

gossip-fart: a fart that encourages others to talk about you behind your back.

global-warming fart: a fart that causes your bath water level to rise significantly.

Grand Canyon fart: a fart that's divided in half at the point of release, usually caused by a pair of really tight thong panties.

Great Wall of China fart: a fart that gains you immediate access to the entire Chinese buffet.

Grinch fart: a fart you found in your Christmas stocking.

guardian-angel fart: a fart that protects you from evildoers.

gumball-machine fart: someone paid you to fart, but now you can't produce anything.

hack fart: a fart that causes your cat to cough up a fur ball.

hangover fart: a fart that causes the whole room to spin.

hallelujah fart: a fart that causes so much internal pressure that a loud "Thank you, God!" is acceptable upon its release.

hallucinatory fart: you know you farted, but there's no aroma lurking, nor is there any reactionary evidence from those around you.

Hamlet fart: any fart emitted while telling a stupid British joke with a cockney accent.

happy-drunk fart: a fart that makes you buy everyone in the bar a round of drinks.

head-start fart: a fart that cuts down your bathroom time.

helium-sucker fart: a fart that sounds like it came from a munchkin from *The Wizard of Oz*.

hesitant fart: a fart cautiously let go a bit at a time for fear of attachments.

Hoffa fart: a fart you won't talk about if you know what's good for you.

hoot-and-coo fart: a fart that encourages mating calls from woodland creatures.

houseguest fart: a fart found in your spare bedroom after company has left.

hula-hoop fart: a fart that seems to keep running rings around you.

I-could-kill-you fart: one of your farts that embarrassed your date at an important social event.

ibuprofen fart: a fart that relieves your intestinal swelling and eases stomach cramps.

identity-crisis fart: a fart that causes you to question your own social identity, because you can't believe the smell that just came out of you.

immaculate fart: a fart while reciting a "Hail Mary" in the front church pew.

immersion fart: a fart for your little brother, who is now locked in the closet of stench.

impasse fart: a fart that serves as a non-penetrative force field, like walking into a glass door.

in-laws fart: a series of well-placed farts that discourage them from staying with you next visit.

inspiration fart: a fart that sparks an insightful new theory on the meaning of life.

island fart: a fart that rids your surrounding area of humans.

Jack Frost fart: a fart let go in subzero weather that seems to have frozen directly below your nostrils.

jackknife fart: this fart can only be released by physically bending at the waist and grabbing on to your ankles.

jacklight fart: a fart used when hunting or fishing at night so your buddies can locate you.

javelin fart: an outdoor fart with distance capability.

jayvee fart: a fart let go during cheerleading tryouts.

Joan Collins fart: a fart that can no longer be transformed into anything recognizable.

joystick fart: a fart let go because you're too lazy to pause the video game and go to the bathroom.

kale fart: a fart with a pungent aroma like that of your aunt Merriam's cabbage stew.

kangaroo fart: a fart with the bizarre ability to leap out of your pants and land many feet away, usually ending up several people ahead of you in the buffet line.

Kardashian fart: a fart you can't keep up with.

karma fart: a fart caused by judgment of another's recent gaseous release.

kernel fart: a fart that smells exactly the same as what you just ate.

kettledrum fart: a fart that can be changed in pitch and/or tone by a subtle adjustment of your rear-end positioning.

kickstand fart: a fart that can only be released by lifting one of your legs while in a standing position.

killjoy fart: a fart that transforms into a very good reason to leave the party immediately.

kinetic-theory fart: a series of two farts in which the first fart rams the second from behind, thus changing its velocity and direction (a great diversionary fart for use during fart battle).

lagoon fart: any fart released while watching a *Gilligan's Island* rerun.

laissez-passer fart: a fart you purposely expel while people are hurriedly passing you by; i.e. subway station, airport, hallway at work.

lap-dog fart: a fart let go with a dog in your lap, which completely exonerates you from any fart suspicion.

last-slice fart: a fart emitted to scare away everyone at the table so you get the last slab of pizza.

lateral fart: a fart you shared with the person behind you.

leisure-suit fart: a fart from a mustached guy at the bar who's stuck in the 1970s.

"Let it go" fart: a fart which causes little girls to freeze in their tracks and sing ceremoniously the same song over and over and over again.

liberated-man fart: a fart from a guy in a sperm-donor waiting room while reading an outdated copy of *Better Homes and Gardens*.

life-stinks fart: any fart let go in the unemployment line; it may also be used in the bank line when depositing your unemployment check.

lightning-rod fart: a fart that has the ability to conduct electricity.

list-of-demands fart: a fart you saved and utilized as a bargaining tool, because your friends know from experience the ramifications of your crappy diet.

litterbox fart: a fart your dog is extremely attracted to.

L'Oréal fart: a fart your friend can't possibly escape because you're coloring her hair (and because she's worth it).

Lucy fart: a fart at the paleontology exhibit that smells only half-human.

lump-of-coal fart: a fart that ruins Christmas.

Machiavellian fart: a fart that instantly raises the social power of the farter, often making them "king for a day."

MacPherson-strut fart: a fart that causes the farter to hover momentarily off their seat.

made-to-order fart: a fart that was intentionally manufactured by the ingestion of certain foods for the sole purpose of future farting.

maestro fart: a fart whose lyrical sound causes the farter to automatically do a quick lift and dip of their arm and pinky finger.

magic-marker fart: a fart that left a stain on your underwear and it won't wash off.

magic-moment fart: a fart emitted during a first kiss that automatically kills all potential for a second kiss.

Magic Mountain fart: a fart from the cheerleader on top of the pyramid.

Man Called Horse fart: a fart from the depressed guy at the bar with the long face.

mass-acre fart: a fart from an altar boy, which causes the priest to stutter and stammer.

mastodon fart: a fart that smells like it's been unearthed after eons of rotting fermentation.

matador fart: a fart you attempt to rid yourself of by casually flapping an apron.

maternity fart: a fart let go during childbirth, causing everyone in the room to wish they'd doubled up on surgical masks.

Matrix fart: a fart that hovers in the air and delivers a kick to the face of the person nearest you.

meteorite fart: a fart so condensed in mass, it feels as if a hole has burned through your underwear.

MIA fart: you know you farted, but now you can't find it.

mistletoe fart: a fart you purposely release so your homely second cousin Millie won't try to kiss you.

Mister Potato Head fart: a fart that makes you wish you could temporarily remove your nose.

musical-chairs fart: a fart that has a noticeable effect on the seating arrangements at the buffet table.

mushroom-omelet fart: an unintentional fart let go at your morning sales meeting that's a clear indication of what you crammed down for breakfast in the hotel lobby.

National Enquirer fart: a fart by Justin Bieber that makes front-page tabloid news.

National Guard fart: a fart delivered during a political event that causes the crowd to disperse in fright, thus resulting in the need of military force out of fear a terrorist act has just been committed.

nativity fart: a fart while in the company of barnyard animals.

nest-egg fart: a fart you've reserved all day for tonight's special occasion.

network fart: a fart used as a communication device.

—▸●◂—

neutered fart: a fart whose composition was drastically altered by the tightness of your underwear.

—▸●◂—

next-exit fart: a fart emitted by a hitchhiker, which immediately calls for a drop-off at the next rest stop.

nice-car fart: a disgusting fart you expel in your friend's new car, as a christening of sorts.

niche fart: a fart that deserves its own literary genre.

Nixon fart: a fart secretly recorded for future embarrassment.

no-vacancy fart: a fart that has saturated the entire room with its foulness, thus rendering the area unfit for humans until further notice.

not-your-fault fart: a fart during an examination by your proctologist.

nun fart: a fart expelled while viewing the penguin exhibit, and harboring bad thoughts about your Catholic upbringing.

octo fart: a fart that's precisely eight times more foul than anything you've ever smelled in your lifetime.

octopus fart: a fart that releases in eight distinct directions.

odyssey fart: a fart that lingers and drifts for what seems like an eternity.

oil-can fart: a slippery fart released one tiny "pop" at a time, for fear of what may be lurking in your bowels if you let it go all at once.

Old MacDonald fart: a fart let go with a *bbrrraaaakkk bbrrraaaakkk* here, and a *bbrrraaaakkk bbrrraaaakkk* there, here a *bbrrraaaakkk*, there a *bbrrraaaakkk* . . .

Omaha fart: a fart let go by an insurance claims officer out of disbelief of the story she's just heard.

opera fart: a fart let loose by the large woman onstage, that lets you know the show's over.

overdue fart: a fart left for your cranky librarian.

overflow fart: a fart that can't be contained in the bath-room, even with the door shut.

pancake-boy fart: a fart from your five-year-old warning you if you don't get him to a bathroom soon, he'll be spending the school day with an Aunt Jemima disc in his pants.

panic-mode fart: a fart signaling you may be in personal danger, and it's probably a good idea to start looking for a bathroom.

patchouli fart: a fart used to cover up your girlfriend's horrible choice of perfume.

peace-on-Earth fart: a fart let go during Christmas midnight Mass with the familiar aroma of the quart of eggnog you drank earlier.

peanut fart: a fart that triggers an allergic

reaction, most frequently hives.

peripheral fart: a fart that causes the corners of your eyes to water.

Philadelphia fart: a fart with a bell sound and a crack in it.

phlegm fart: a fart expelled while coughing.

photocopier fart: a fart left in the copy room at work, and the machine is out of paper or toner, resulting in the next poor soul having to remedy the problem amid your gassy haze.

picnic-basket fart: a fart that attracts bears.

plastic-surgeon fart: you thought the large-breasted woman in front of you farted, but no, it was just her Double Ds rubbing together.

Polly fart: a fart you've taught your bird to imitate.

Poltergeist fart: a ghastly fart that can haunt a home for generations.

pope fart: a fart with the aroma of really bad incense.

portrait fart: a fart that eerily follows you everywhere you go.

pot-o'-gold fart: a fart from a short Irishman cashing in his lottery ticket.

preppie fart: a neat and tidy fart left in a Fifth Avenue dressing room.

privileged fart: a fart shared with you from a person of entitlement.

Publisher's Clearing House fart: a fart you may have already emitted.

pump fart: a fart used to puff up your inflatable doll.

quaalude fart: a disabling fart that causes you to crumble to the floor in a jerky motion (most popular at discos across the globe in the 1970s).

quarantine fart: a fart that has to be left in the room with the door shut.

quarter-pounder fart: a fart that smells like an old McDonald's hamburger.

quartermaster fart: a fart delivered by the fart leader that signals the beginning of a fart contest. (Note: The quartermaster fart is not to be included in judging; rather, it is only to be used as a signaling device to commence the duel.)

queen-substance fart: a fart expelled by a senior sorority member during initiation that causes all the freshman pledges to giggle and fart uncontrollably.

rabbit fart: a fart with a stench that multiplies rapidly.

rabid fart: a fart that causes your little brother to gag and spit up his oatmeal.

racetrack fart: a fart that circles the room, but eventually returns to its original starting point.

Raisin Bran fart: a breakfast-table fart with two scoops of foulness.

raisin-in-the-sun fart: a fart while touring a vineyard.

Ralph Kramden fart: any fart let go on a city bus.

recipe fart: a fart of your own that you enjoyed so much, you must write down what your previous meal was so you can repeat that fart in the future.

reluctant fart: you have to fart, but if you stand and exit you risk the possibility of a "walk and release," so you take your chances while sitting and let go a little at a time.

REM fart: a fart that you thought was part of a dream, but by the look on your partner's face it appears to have been authentic.

right-of-way fart: a bold series of farts emitted in succession while traversing a crowded nightclub.

rip-off fart: a fart that's worth more than you were paid for it.

Ruskie fart: a fart shared while drinking good vodka and discussing bad politics.

'73 Pinto fart: fart in a car with inoperable windows.

Schuster fart: a celebratory fart upon signing a publishing contract.

security fart: an airport fart that gets you passed over for a strip search.

Seven Dwarfs fart: any series of tiny farts that follow a large fart.

Sharon Stone fart: a fart while crossing your legs.

Sheldon fart: a fart that knocks three times on your sphincter before release.

showcase fart: though almost impossible, this fart is worthy of framing.

silent fart: a fart from a mime.

silhouette fart: a fart so dense, it has a shadow.

skip-dessert fart: a fart that has ruined dinner.

slushie fart: a fart that causes you to have a brain freeze.

snail fart: a fart that creeps across the room at a very slow pace.

soufflé fart: a fart so warm and gaseous that it rises immediately, hopefully making its way to the guest bedroom upstairs.

"sounds like" fart: a fart used as a clue during a drunken game of charades.

squirrel fart: a bushy fart you have to waggle out of your pants.

static fart: a fart that makes the hair of everyone in the room stand on end.

stay-in-bed fart: a fart that confirms there's something very wrong with your intestines, and it's wise to call in sick.

Stephen King fart: a fart that scares the crap out of you.

Stock Exchange fart: a joyous fart while making a ridiculously good trade on Wall Street.

strike-a-pose fart: a fart in which you fear a personal explosion if you make even the slightest move.

subliminal fart: a fart that mysteriously changes the topic of discussion from politics to bad food.

sunscreen fart: a fart that gets caught in your beach umbrella.

sushi fart: an underwater fart that attracts fish.

Swan Lake fart: any fart ejected while wearing leotards.

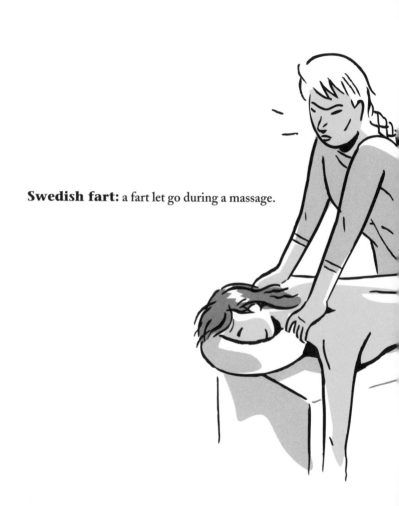

Swedish fart: a fart let go during a massage.

tassel fart: a windy fart that causes the tassels on your New Year's Eve dress to seem like they're blowing in the wind.

tattoo fart: a fart that chemically reacts with your underwear, and now you have red heart prints planted semipermanently on your cheeks.

tea-cake fart: a small, thin fart that smells like raisins.

telemarketing fart: a fart let go over the phone for the guy trying to sell you a timeshare in Wisconsin.

Templar fart: a fart that hovers near your rear to protect and defend the "Holy Sphincter."

Tempurpedic fart: a fart that goes unnoticed by your bedmate.

tether-ball fart: a fart that orbits around the farter.

That's-a-nice-sweater fart: a fart which you must, without delay, cover up by complimenting the person with whom you're conversing.

theater-of-war fart: a fart slowly let go around the perimeter of the fart grounds to establish the competition boundary.

"therefore I am" fart: a fart at a social function that gets you noticed when you'd have otherwise spent the entire evening gathering no attention whatsoever.

Tom Brady fart: a barely traceable fart but results in you not being allowed to play outside with your friends for six weeks.

three-legged fart: a fart that feels as if it's tethered to your leg.

Twitter fart: a fart that delivers exactly 140 characteristics of smell.

ugly-truth fart: a fart that confirms the suspicion that your girlfriend is not the delicate flower you thought she was.

uncomfortable fart: a fart that causes you to walk like your underwear is stuck in your crack.

uncool fart: any fart emitted while wearing plaid.

undaunted fart: a fart discharged as an act of bravery, such as farting in the direction of a brown bear in Yosemite in hopes of scaring the beast away.

underboss fart: a celebratory fart from the guy who didn't get indicted.

underhand fart: a fart you waft away from your butt with a palm out, upward swing of your hand.

United Way fart: a fart you give to another without expecting anything in return.

upgrade-your-plan fart: a fart you're so vehemently proud of, you must phone someone long distance and tell them about it.

upstream fart: a fart that smells like salmon are spawning in a nearby room.

U.S. Open fart: a fart let go by a golfer at the very moment he hits the best drive of his life, so he immediately glares at the caddy to transfer the fart blame.

vagabond fart: a fart that doesn't lose any of its aromatic power as it wafts from person to person, usually settling in a dark corner of the room.

valet fart: a fart left in your car by the parking attendant because of the cheap tip you gave him.

valley fart: a fart you leaked out in your friend's sunken living room, and you pray it won't make it into the foyer, where your blind date just arrived.

varmint fart: a fart that smells like you're hiding road kill in your pocket.

veg-o-matic fart: a fart that slices to shreds the engaging conversation you were having.

Velcro fart: a fart you can't get off you without drawing attention to yourself.

virgin-in-the-volcano fart: a fart from the only female at the Super Bowl party.

VO5 fart: a fart released in the shower while shampooing your hair.

Walking Dead fart: a fart that sends you on a lengthy search for more of the vile you recently ingested.

wardrobe-change fart: a fart that makes you second-guess the white outfit you were planning on wearing this evening.

watermelon fart: a fart that attracts flies during a summer cookout.

weed-killer fart: a fart that causes nearby foliage to wilt or die.

welcome-mat fart: a fart you expel after ringing the doorbell, but before your host answers the door.

"Well, uh" fart: a fart let go during a hesitation period while trying to make a moot point.

what's-forn-lunch fart: a fart that has traveled over a cubicle wall in a professional office setting.

whistle-blower fart: a fart by an individual who immediately blames another for his fart.

who-cares fart: a fart from a senior citizen.

widescreen fart: a fart in which your chances of escaping the area without notice are exactly 1.33:1.

X-chromosome fart: a fart that may possibly affect the genetic makeup of the person next to you.

X-Files fart: a fart that is not of this world.

X-ray fart: a fart that can be seen through your underwear.

xylophone fart: a long and varied tonal fart that produces the entire musical scale.

yeti fart: a fart explosion from fear alone because your camping buddy has just appeared outside your tent wearing a palmetto wig, and he's suffering from a three-day beer buzz.

Yo Yo Ma fart: a fart that sounds like you have an out-of-tune cello in your pants.

yolk-stalk fart: a fart that feels like it's still connected to internal tissue.

young-and-foolish fart: a fart by a pubescent male in front of a small group of cheerleaders who have him cornered at his locker.

yuletide fart: a fart that covers up the fresh Christmas tree aroma.

zapper fart: a fart with the ability to repel mosquitoes.

zebra fart: a fart let go while eating a black-and-white cookie.

zeppelin fart: a dinnertime fart that catches the tablecloth on fire.

Ziggy fart: a fart that barely peeks out the back of your pants.

zinfandel fart: a fart released at a wine tasting whose aroma makes everyone feel tipsy.

zodiac fart: a fart shared with another person of the same sign, while discussing all the similar traits you have.

zone-refining fart: a fart that picks up additional aroma as it passes through your two-day-old underwear.

zonk fart: a fart that makes your dog roll over and play dead.

zombie fart: a fart whose smell seems to return to life with renewed vigor every few minutes.